Edward King

Considerations on the Utility of the National Debt

And on the present alarming crisis, with a short plan of a mode of relief

Edward King

Considerations on the Utility of the National Debt
And on the present alarming crisis, with a short plan of a mode of relief

ISBN/EAN: 9783337378097

Printed in Europe, USA, Canada, Australia, Japan

Cover: Foto ©ninafisch / pixelio.de

More available books at **www.hansebooks.com**

CONSIDERATIONS

ON THE

UTILITY

OF THE

NATIONAL DEBT:

AND ON THE

PRESENT ALARMING CRISIS;

WITH

A SHORT PLAN OF A MODE OF RELIEF,

AND AN

EXPLANATION OF THE SOLID INHERENT GROUNDS OF
GREAT NATIONAL PROSPERITY, THAT EXIST
IN THIS COUNTRY.

By EDWARD KING, Esq. F.R.S. and F.A.S.

Ne aut temere defperet, propter ignaviam ; aut
nimis confidat, propter cupiditatem.————
Cic. de Officiis, L. 1. S. 21.

`LONDON;
PRINTED FOR T. PAYNE, MEWS-GATE.

1793.

ADVERTISEMENT
TO THE READER.

———————

IT is not any conceited desire of obtruding new ideas upon the Public, that has induced me to venture this pamphlet into the world; but a sincere wish to afford, if possible, some little assistance to my Country, in time of necessity; by communicating the result of long and deep reflections;—which those whom it more immediately concerns may make such use of as they think fit.

A man who has been accustomed to think MOST INTENTLY on a few subjects, is inclined to do so on all.—And such an habit of INTENT THINKING has long caused me to view many thing *things in a light somewhat different from popular apprehensions and prejudices.*

I therefore deem it an indispensable duty, at least to make my ideas known ; if there may only be A POSSIBILITY *of their becoming serviceable, even in the least degree, to those in any departments, to whom such ideas, for want of such habit, may not have occurred.*

That long and close attention which I have for so many years bestowed in the pursuit of Philosophical enquiries ; in the investigation of the most serious subjects ; and in searching out the progress of arts, and improvements, in successive ages ; may perhaps be found to have given occasion to reflections, that may be useful in this VERY CRITICAL ÆRA; *when the advance of increasing arts and improvements is become at last so rapid, that the machine of the Body Politic can scarce sustain the violence of the rapidity.*

EDWARD KING.

Mansfield-street,
May 16 1793.

CONSIDERATIONS

ON THE

UTILITY.

OF THE

NATIONAL DEBT.

———————

EVERY one who is acquainted with the history of this country, during this laſt century, well knows, that the moſt general ſubject of Parliamentary Declamation, in times of emergency; and the moſt frequent cauſe of vulgar and popular alarm and apprehenſion, has been *the magnitude of the National Debt :—*from the time that the lay-

B   ing

ing such a *firm foundation for Public Credit, and for Private Prosperity*, was first ventured upon, *as a matter of mere necessity*, to this very hour. And the alarm, and pretended danger, it may be observed, was no less, but even greater, when the sum amounted to no more than a few millions; than it has been even in these latter days, when we have had the supposed danger arising from a weight of so many millions, continually and loudly sounded in our ears.

Yet all this time we have found ourselves, by the unmerited mercy and blessing of Almighty God, notwithstanding this outcry, in a state of great prosperity and plenty: far beyond that which existed *before the funding system was adopted.* A prosperity that has continued, and is still likely to continue; surmounting even the dreadful shock to credit in general, which the speculation of interested individuals (too long unheeded by Government) has now at length occasioned;

in

in confequence of their venturing to raife *an additional loan upon the public*, of fuch enormous bulk, as even to bear no inconfiderable proportion to that of the *National Debt*; without any adequate funds ; and, indeed, in many inftances, almoft without any funds at all to fupport it.

There muft, therefore, exift fome truly rational caufe for this long profperity, and for fuch ftable fupport ; notwithftanding thofe received popular prejudices, which have occafioned a great National Debt to be conftantly condemned, as being the means of great National danger; and the fact muft, in reality, be quite otherwife than has been fo *generally* apprehended.

It is, I am perfuaded, fo much otherwife; that the real matter of aftonifhment, to a penetrating and confiderate mind, ought rather to have been ;— — not that public credit was, from time to time, ftill firmly *eftablifhed*, and even extended under the con-

duct

duct of different administrations;—nor that
the *Public Debt* has even born *increafe*,
without any mifchievous effects being actually
produced ;— — — but rather that the continual perfect *fafety* of *Public fecurities*, during
a long fucceffion of events, for an hundred
years (many of which were fully fufficient to
have undermined their ftability, had there
not been an *unfufpected* fupport founded in
the true reafon of things), that this continued
fafety and ftability, fhould never have opened
the eyes of a fedate thinking people ; or have
removed their unfounded prejudices ; fo as to
convince them that there had been a grofs
miftake in their prior reafonings upon this
fubject ;---which were indeed originally only
founded |in the whifperings of interefted
partizans.

A miftake there certainly was ;— *popular* ;
and *contrived* to miflead : and one great caufe
of it was, the mifchief arifing from the mere
imperfection of language, and the not properly

perly diftinguifhing different things, called by the fame name; and therefore from the confounding *the nature of* what was called, *a Public Debt*, with that of *a Private Debt*: which latter is indeed, moft truly, ever ruinous in its own nature.

In confequence of this confufion of ideas, by fuch a mere fimilitude of names; it was concluded, that the effects of *a debt*; fo called in both inftances, muft be juft the fame. --- Whereas, when the matter is clofely confidered, with regard to their immediate operations, and ftill more, when the remote confequences are duly taken into confideration, no two things can be more widely different, or more oppofite in their effects, than a *Public*, and a *Private Debt*. For a *Public Debt* may even moft truly *be called a Public Support*. And this country has really received (as I am perfuaded every perfon of reflection will allow, when the matter is duly weighed) more benefit *from the very exiftence*

of

of the Debt alone simply, for this laſt century;
than from any of thoſe vaſt efforts, or im-
portant cauſes, which, unavoidably, occa-
ſioned either the firſt beginning of it ; or the
increaſing of it.

To a contemplative mind, this, I truſt,
will in the end be moſt obvious : as all thoſe
very peculiar circumſtances of our long prof-
perous ſituation ; and that moſt remarkable
chain of events which took place ſoon after
the introducing the funding ſyſtem ; and on
which the public proſperity, by the bleſſing
and merciful goodneſs of Divine Providence,
is at preſent founded ; do moſt fully prove it.

For no ſooner did the Public Debt *begin*
to be funded, than a totally new, unexpected,
and *quite unheeded ſum*, to a great amount,
was annually flung into circulation ; for the
encouragement of the induſtrious ; and for
the benefit of the poor artificer. This ſum
was, neither more nor leſs, than *the annual
intereſt paid* for what was called the Debt :

which

which fum it was impoffible for the ftockholders either to annihilate, or to hoard up
(except for a very fhort time) ; and which,
therefore, *from this period,* conftantly went
forth, either to furnifh the neceffaries, or to
procure the indulgences of civilized life ;
and became an hidden fource of fupply to
every tradefman, and to every member of
fociety, who was endeavouring to get an
honeft livelihood by ingenious and com-
mendable employment in various branches,
either of mechanical labour, of agriculture,
and cultivation of all kinds, or of manufacturing.

This fum, when paid *annually* by Government, did not (like the intereft of *a mere
Private Debt*) *depart* from its owner *for
ever,* as a real diminution of property; and as
an expenditure never to be made amends for :
—but, if the Public was to be confidered as
the debtor, and as paying this intereft (as
was moft certainly the cafe), it even *remained
ftill employed for the advantage of the original
poffeffor* ;

poffeffor; only in a different form, and under circumftances rendering it ftill more ufeful to that original poffeffor than it had been before ; it being now *in continual circulation.*

And whilft, from the beginning of this century, to this day, feffion after feffion, thofe who thought themfelves moft interefted in the welfare of this country, were declaiming, in Parliament, againft *the danger of the National Debt*; and foretelling the ruin they believed muft needs enfue ; and whilft every poffeffor of perfonal property in the funds was continually trembling for the rifk that was fancied to be run ; yet it came to pafs, in the natural courfe of things (though moft ftrangely in contradiction to popular prejudices, and to the great aftonifhment of all), that, on every emergency, the Public Debt was *eafily increafed*, without any real lofs to individuals ; and even ftill more encouragement was found continually to be given, on every fuch exertion, to every fpecies of home manufacture ; and more, people continually found a means

of

of obtaining an honeſt livelihood, and to
have wherewith to pay eaſily ſtill more and
greater taxes.—And, at laſt, after ſuch an
accumulation of Public Debt, as our anx-
ious anceſtors never believed to be poſſible,
the nation appeared in *a more proſperous
ſituation* than before; and the increaſe of
buildings, in almoſt every city and town, and
eſpecially in the metropolis; and the increaſe
of artizans of all ſorts; plainly ſhewed, that
there was ſtill, in reality, no impoveriſhment
of the community; nor any want of ſupply
to the calls of induſtrious individuals.

In ſhort, *the progreſs of the increaſe of the
National Debt, and the danger of the miſchief
enſuing from it, has been very ſimilar to the
mathematical progreſs of the Hyperbola and its
Ordinate: they never have met; nor ever can
meet;* as the increaſe of the former adds ſuch
aſſiſtances and ſupports to individuals to pay
taxes, as will probably for ever prevent, the
approach of the latter; unleſs Government
loſe their uſual prudence.

C   This

(10)

This may appear, at first fight, to ordinary reafoners, problematical; and even parodoxical: but to mature confideration; to a mind capable of deep and folid reafoning, nothing can furely be plainer, or more confiftent with truth.

The folution of the whole difficulty lies merely in inveftigating *a very obvious matter of fact*; which the prejudices of mankind have yet been unwilling to attend to.

The whole of the riches, of any country on earth, depends upon, and folely confifts in, *the produce of the earth; the produce of ingenuity, and of the improvement of rational faculties; and the produce of induftry.* But this produce, be it (by the Divine gift) great or fmall, is not a quantum of riches at any time capable of being hoarded up in chefts as it is acquired; or fuch as can be returned to the earth, and buried therein: but is a continual *annual growth*, to be annually ufed: and therefore is, and ought to be confidered only as *the mere* INTEREST

of

of a vaſt ideal capital.—A capital, which, inſtead of being called *the Public Debt*, ſhould rather be called *the Public Ability*, by a more right uſe of language.—A capital, which never did exiſt as one great *lump* of *gold*, or *clay*; or as a *great treaſure of money*, to be actually ſubdivided into a certain number of parts : nor ever ought ſo to exiſt.—But yet which is not, according to the vulgar expreſſion, *merely in the clouds*; but does exiſt ſubſtantially, and moſt effectually, in the real gifts of God to the country.—In the abilities and honeſt exertions of multitudes of induſtrious perſons. A ſubſtantial treaſure far better than mere hoards of gold : but a treaſure which, in order to be enjoyed, muſt have the opportunity offered of thoſe *abilities and exertions* being *fully* employed : which they cannot be, unleſs a ſufficient quantity of floating intereſt, created by and properly belonging to what is called the *Public Debt*, be kept in continual circulation. For ſhould the

quantum

quantum of such interest at any time be, in the whole, too much diminished; or be checked in its circulation: or should numbers of private families, whose property is vested in the public funds, by any diminution of their annual income, cease to be enabled to make the *usual calls* for the various necessaries, or conveniences, or even luxuries of life; the employment of thousands and ten thousands of people, whose subsistence depends on the trades and avocations supported by *such calls*, must cease; and the abilities and exertions of the multitude, that were before so fully and usefully drawn forth, will become *dormant*.

It is, therefore, perhaps, by no means too bold a conclusion to affirm, that, instead of being terrified with those false fears, which of late have had such undue weight and encouragement given to them; we might even justly venture now to consider, whether the *National Debt* is not so far from being a public

public evil; that it might even in future be increafed, on fome proper occafion, with the utmoft advantage to the whole community, in every clafs of life.

Candid reflection, and long obfervation, may fairly lead us to conclude, that it may fafely be fo increafed; and even advantage-oufly to every individual, as well as to the Public; till the whole of the *Nominal Ideal Capital* fhall be fuch, as to call forth annu-ally, as the mere annual circulating intereft thereof, the whole produce of the land; the whole effect of manufacturing mechanic art; and all thofe efforts of the induftrious, in every clafs, which fupply families with every neceffary and convenience of life.

Till fuch a full adjuftment of the annual intereft, to the Great Ideal Capital, of the *National Debt*, or rather of the *National Abi-lity*, fhall have taken place, I am perfuaded every noify alarm is juft as much without foundation now, as it was the firft day when

the

the funding fyftem was fo happily introduced into the world.

And fuch a period of *adjuftment* probably *will never arrive.* Becaufe the continued and increafing encouragement offered to induftry and ingenuity, and the frefh demands of all kinds of fupplies of provifions, and conveniences, for houfeholds (whofe numbers muft by this very means be conftantly increafing), will moft likely ever be *in juft as progreffive a ftate* as the increafe of the *Ideal* Capital itfelf in confequence of the continual additional *funding.* Provided only, the increafe of funding be made *with caution :* at proper times : and merely as the increafed ability of the members of the community will admit. And provided the taxation confequent thereupon, be contrived to be clofely connected with the actual circulation of the intereft. Which latter *provifo* there are means of effecting.

Now let us turn our attention, and confider the converfe of thefe ideas.——

Had

Had the ancient apprehenfions of our fore-
fathers, and their ftrong prejudices, been able
to accomplifh the object of their wifhes, *the
paying off the National Debt,* in any early
period of its exiftence ; they had not only, in
truth, with-held from the prefent generation
the comfortable increafed means of fupport
and employment to thoufands and ten thoufands of honeft and induftrious perfons, in all
the various branches of trade; but would
themfelves have almoft inftantly experienced
moft mifchievous effects, without at all ap-
prehending the caufe: for they would not
merely have been in *the fame* fituation
they were (as to employment for the induftrious part of the community) before
the funding of the Debt began; but
would have found all thofe numerous *additional families,* who had lately obtained a
comfortable fubfiftence, by means of the late
increafed circulation of property, become
very rapidly deftitute of their ufual fupport,
and of their conftant employment: and *thefe*

muft

muſt either have been provided for by a re-
vival of thoſe vaſt herds of Retainers, and De-
pendants, attending the Manſions of the
Great as in former times ; and by a Reſtoration
of ſomething ſimilar to the ancient Refectories
of monaſteries, and religious houſes ; where
ſo many idle paupers were entertained : or
elſe the unemployed muſt have been ſuffered
to remain in their ſtate of indigence, till
their neceſſities prompted them to all manner of violence and plunder.

And if, in theſe latter ages, either the
falſe alarms ſpread ; or the inſidious deſigns
of any who are deſirous to create confuſion ;
or the miſtakes of any adminiſtration ; or the
blundering eager wiſhes of ſelfiſh perſons,
not poſſeſſed of any valuable property ; could
affect either an overthrow of the *public funds*,
or a diminution of the quantum of intereſt
paid, and of the money which is thereby
annually flung into circulation; the conſe-
quence wou'd ſoon be, not merely the private
loſs of each individual ſtockholder (moſt

of

of whom would perhaps find means of fubfifting, although with hardfhip, and in a re-
duced ftate); but it would become *the abfolute
annihilation of the means of obtaining bread to
all the poorer and induftrious part of the community*; who would ceafe to have their ufual
employment, whenever the numerous ftockholders, now fubfifting, ceafed to be able to
purchafe thofe neceffaries, and thofe indulgences, and comforts of life (that are pur-
chafed, in fo many inftances, almoft folely by
the annual income received from the public
funds). Yet thefe unhappy, induftrious men,
would, from miftake, on any fuch event, ever
be too prone to fall to murmuring, and riot-
ing; and into a ftate of dire confufion. And
as this would be the confequence of a *total
fubverfion of the funds*, or of any confiderable
diminution of the intereft continually in circulation; fo, even *the fair* paying off *of any*
GREAT *part of the Public Debt*, would, I
may be bold to affirm, be no real advantage:
but would, in a certain proportion, caufe a
degree of *ftagnation* of employment for the

inferior

inferior branches of mankind, that would be moſt ſeverely felt ; and would *render the payment of the taxes* THAT STILL REMAINED, *much more an objeƈt of complaint than before any were taken off*; and would make it ſtill more difficult, on any emergency, to raiſe *freſh ſupplies*; or to exert *the Public Ability* with energy.

It can never be too often repeated, that the *general vaſt circulation* of the money paid as public intereſt, is that which principally enables all orders and ranks of men to pay the neceſſary taxes with eaſe, and to obtain ſuch degrees of property as to contribute to freſh ſupplies. Nor ſhould we ever loſe ſight of the conſideration, that the various induſtrious employments, ariſing from *this circulation of the public intereſt from the funds,* will ever increaſe faſter than the taxes drawn from the perſons ſo obtaining a livelihood, can poſſibly do : if proper prudence be but uſed by Government, as to *the times* of raiſing ſuch ſupplies, and the *degrees of their quantum*; and as to the *method of rendering each*

ſource

source of revenue permanent; and as to ·the
mode of taxation; *that it may always as nearly
as possible accompany the increased circulation.*

The mischiefs surely that would have en-
sued from annihilating the National Debt;
or from taking any considerable part of the
interest paid for it, *out* of circulation; are
from all these considerations sufficiently manifest : and we can surely no longer avoid
perceiving, that multitudes have actually
found employment since its existence, who
did not do so before ; and who could not
have found that employment, but for the
creation and existence of such debt.

And as far as experiment can go, in point
of fact, we may add ; that those persons who
lived at the time, and were free from prejudices of party, or narrow self-interest ; and
who were either in such situations, and of
such penetration and abilities, as rendered
them capable of making just observations;
must have been aware, what an *unexpected
and mischievous sort of stagnation, as to the
emoluments of the industrious poor*, the inju-

dicious

dicious ftep of lowering the public interefl, on the fuggeftion of Sir John Bernard, occafioned in almoft every part of the kingdom ; and muft remember that event with great concern : and efpecially as none of the bene-fits expected ever refulted from that ftep.

Befides the affirmation of all thefe plain facts, concerning the utility of the circula-tion occafioned by the intereft of the Public Funds, it may alfo be added; that all the prejudices exifting in the minds of thofe who wifh for the annihilation of the National Debt; or for the diminution of its circulating intereft ; are founded in falfehood *and error.*

For, in the firft place, it may be obferved, the poffeffor of *landed property* would be by no means benefited by any fuch event and meafures : fince long and repeated experience has now fhewn, with regard to the real value even of *that fpecies of property; that the price of land has, upon the whole, ever rifen greatly in every county, from the time of the firft com-mencement of the National Debt.* And when-ever the funds have been in their moft depreffed fituation; and whenever the world at large have, by mifreprefentations, been injurioufly led to have the worft opinion of *their* fecurity; *the price of land* (inftead of rifing, from the fuppofed fuperior advantage of landed poffeffions, as one would expect it fhould do) *has always fallen* in the greateft degree.

And with regard to the value of *the produce* of land; and *the rents* at which land will let to the tenant; it may alfo be obferved, nothing can be more certain, than that the *great confumption of every kind of produce of land* is greatly increafed by thofe many working hands and tradefmen, who live by means of the increafed circulation of money, arifing from the various expences of *thofe who receive the National Intereft*. And if that fource was once dried up in any confiderable degree;——whilft the poor workman ftarved for want of his ufual employ, the landlord muft lofe his rent for want of the tenant finding the ufual market. And it is utterly impoffible to conceive, that any improvement, or further cultivation

tivation of land whatever, could in any shape produce *such additional demand for the produce* of the fruits of the earth; or such a means of paying a good price for them; as would at all make good the deficiency: whilst, as to any fancied increase of commerce, or of trade, that should occasion a similar demand; from what quarter imaginable could it so surely proceed as from the present cause? Or who can be so weak as to think, that commerce should flourish more, under the diminished *home consumption* of every article of life, and under the depressure men must feel from finding property, when acquired, of so much less value? Or that persons who are backward to trust their money with commercial persons, on *private security,* NOW, whilst such commercial persons are careful to give the best security they can find; would trust it with *them,* when money should be (as the enemies of the public funds wish it to be) to merchants a mere drug.

In the next place; as to those, who it is erroneously supposed would *be relieved,* by

having the payment of taxes removed from
their shoulders, when the National Debt
should be, in any confiderable degree, either
paid off, or annihilated : nothing can be
more manifeft, than that *the being eafed from
paying land-tax, houfe-tax, window-tax, and
the taxes on all the little various articles of
houfekeeping (whatever they are), would be no
recompence for the lofs of trade and employment,*
to the induftrious part of the community
(who are by far the moft numerous); and
would be of no fort of benefit to the *reft,* in
proportion to the advantages they would lofe,
as to the improvement or ufes of their property of any kind.

And laftly, with regard to Government
itfelf : fo far would *it be* from being benefited
by the paying off the whole, or a great part
of the Public Debt ; that there is every reafon
to believe, that in confequence of the *gradual
ftagnation,* which muft arife *from the want of
the ufual circulation,* it would be fo far from
being an eafier matter to raife a new fupply,
on any preffing occafion; or to levy any new

or

orf refh taxes, in the room of thofe laid afide, on paying off the debt; that the very attempt to do fo, would create more uneafinefs than any the greateft augmentation of the debt has ever yet done, or can do; and that the attempt to levy any taxes at all then, would be attended with moie danger of inquietude than ever.

We may, therefore, confider the *Public Debt*, as it is too often malicioufly called; to be rather a wonderful and moft advantageous mode of creation *of public ftrength and confidence, and of public advantage*; by throwing all the riches proceeding from the produce of the land, the produce of the induftry, and the produce of the honeft ingenuity of the country, into perpetual circulation; inftead of fuffering them, when produced, to moulder away, or to be laid by as an ufelefs hoard, or buried in a ftate of torpid ftagnation.

And that indeed the Public Debt has in reality, at all times, been *capable* of a ftill further *increafe*, beyond all common apprehenfion, is obvious, from what has actually *filently* taken place of late years.

For whilft men have been unjuftly murmuring; and complaining of the danger of funding; and talking of the impoffibility to Government of proceeding further in raifing fupplies; private individuals have actually raifed fupplies; raifed *a further fund* upon the Public; which even bears no fmall proportion to that raifed by Government itfelf.—The Fund I mean, is that raifed by *Provincial Bankers,* to a vaft amount; without proper means in general, for its fupport.—The fad inconvenience of permitting this is now at laft too deeply felt. And for the fake of preventing this, indeed, thefe very remarks were orlginally penned : but through an unwillingnefs to interfere unneceffarily, they were not publifhed in their original form ; hoping the evil might cure itfelf.

Mifchievous as the effect is now become; yet it muft ftill be confeffed, that even the raifing of this vaft additional fund, fo much without

E   fupport,

support, was, for a time, so far from being injurious to the community, that it was even of great advantage to it. But yet surely the matter ought to have been sooner attended to : and the whole advantage, (so enticing to those who could not support the undertaking) ought to have been to Government; instead of being to private individuals, who were thus misled. And the security ought to have been *from* Government: in which case all had been safe.

No sooner did a Provincial banker (possessed at first perhaps but of small capital) think of adopting that plan of business, for the convenience of the neighbouring country; *(for so in reality it was)* ; than he procured a few books of *neatly* engraved cash notes, for the payment *of five pounds, or five guineas each*;—the leaves of which books (having first signed them properly) he proceeded to cut out; and then got them very soon into circulation; to the amount of fifty, or sixty thousand pounds: either

in

return for cafh paid into his fhop; or by
means of engaging in various branches of
merchandize.

And no fooner was this done, than he inftantly
deemed himfelf worth that fum : depending
upon the being able to keep thofe notes in
perpetual circulation. For fo long as he
could do *that*, he might difpofe of the cafh
paid in, juft as he pleafed.

In this ftrange manner; to the utter aftonifhment of all who before knew him; many
a man has profeffedly become worth prodi-
gious fums on a fudden. Manifefting plainly
to the world that he was fo; by actually
purchafing land; or ftock in the public funds;
or elfe vefting property on private fecurities,
to fuch amount. And, in truth, fo long as he
could keep thofe notes in *perpetual circulation*; (which, from the convenience of them
to the country round, he had almoft reafon to
flatter himfelf would be for ever), no kind
of property acquired could appear more ftable
or permanent

There was hardly an inftance, for feveral

E 2

years

years, in any one of the Cities or Towns in England, of any one of thofe Provincial bankers having failed; or even of his having been in danger : although it was well known fome of them did not ftand clear of engaging in branches of bufinefs, in which merchants, under other circumftances, have often failed. for fome of the very means, by which certain of thefe perfons have effected the getting their cafh-notes the more rapidly into circulation, has been; their becoming themfelves, all at once, timber merchants; corn merchants; miners, and tinners; or very adventurous manufacturers.

Thus, by an undertaking, which, when ftrictly and clofely analyfed, is in its original really neither more nor lefs than a fpecies of *coining* *, has a fum of many millions been raifed upon the Public; *over and*

. * The fame kind of mifchief exactly, only in a much more formidable degree, has now arifen from the permitting *the coinage of country bankers five pound notes*; that arofe formerly, in a fmaller degree, in confequence of permitting to country tradefmen, *the actual coinage of money*;

and above the sum total of the National Debt.
For all the total amount of the principal
sums possessed by the numerous, and now so
long professedly rich Provincial bankers, is
really only an *additional public fund: an
additional supply drawn from the Public :* the
exceeding utility of which, if it had but
been founded on a fair and just support of
substantial funds, would have been most
manifest; instead of our experiencing any such
injury from it, as we have now perceived.—
Most true it is, that without the help
of this very mode of increased circulation,
there would long ago have been a most
mischievous stagnation in every County
in England ; just such as we unhappily find
there is now. And the payment of rents, as
well as the negotiation of business, would have
still sooner become a matter of great difficulty.
Besides which, there would have been, for

by means of their being permitted to issue forth, what
were called *Tradesmen's Tokens* ; the vast variety, and
numbers of which, and their once general circulation, is
well known to the curious.

want

want of thefe banking notes, a moft horrible
increafe and influx of thofe fort of dangerous
negotiable bills, the uncertainty of the-
fecurity of which has often occafioned fo
many bankruptcies; and has afforded fo terrible
an opportunity of fraud.

Another confiderable fum, funded upon the
Public, has been, *that* raifed for the making
and fupporting the feveral turnpikes, and
canals in the kingdom. And I might indeed
mention very many others befides.

Yet all thefe new funds have ftill been
found advantageous (in many refpects) in their
effects. What then is the conclufion? Why,
plainly, that an increafe of funds there *muft be*
in fome fhape or other, if property is to be
maintained.

And that, in fhort, in the regular courfe
and nature of things, all property is verging
towards the becoming, openly, and clearly,
what the deepeft reafoning and reflection
will teach us it muft in its very propereft
effence be: that is, *a matter only of exact and*
regular

regular PUBLIC ACCOUNT. *The whole*
ANNUAL PRODUCE *of the country, in every*
shape, BEING FLUNG AT LAST INTO
CIRCULATION, BY WAY OF MERE IN-
TEREST OF A NOMINAL CAPITAL; *and*
the property, and the right of each individual,
to his share of the vast principal, corresponding
to his share of the interest, being secured BY A
POSITIVE CLEAR ACCOUNT, *like that of the*
Bank, and of Bankers; subject to no prevarica-
tion or deceit : but for ever under the public eye,
and open to the fairest inspection.

The whole *annual income* of every man's
property, in whatever shape it may have been
vested, ought perhaps, in the eye of truth,
justice, and reason, to become as accurately
a stated account, under the eye of Government;
as his expenditure at his private banker's
now is, under the eye of each banking house;
and as his present possession of any share in
the funds is, under the eye of the bank.

Whenever this vast idea concerning the sta-
bility of property is realized in practice; which
I am persuaded it will and must undoubtedly
in

be in the end: either by gradual steps arising from *mere neceffity*; fimilar to thofe whereby the funding fyftem has firft been made known; or elfe by means of wife and cautious operations and plans of Government: when once this is brought to pafs: it will effectually put a ftop to thofe formidable evils, that have hitherto been fo injurious to the community; *the poffibility of bankruptcies; and of frauds, either in titles to eftates,* or with regard to the Public finances; and even to the poffibility of forgeries.

To explain all this; (although it may be fully and accurately done, upon the moft mathematical principles), would not only *now* be premature; but would render thefe obfervations too tedious; and be moreover *beyond the immediate purpofe of them*:—which is; after having previoufly fhewn the firm foundation of what I have ventured to affert as a matter of the utmoft import, namely, *that the National Debt is* NO INJURY; *ought not to be* MATERIALLY LESSENED; *and may, even with advantage to the whole community, be* HEREAFTER INCREASED); to fuggeft to the public confideration, in the end, a few thoughts concerning the methods that may be ufed to reftore a free and confidential circulation of bills and notes: and to recover, with increafed benefit to the whole community, and to Government, *the advantage* hitherto fo fadly *loft*, by permitting Provincial bankers virtually to fund fuch immenfe fums of money:—of which funding, Government itfelf ought to have had the original benefit on the one hand; and to have rendered the effect *fafe to every individual* on the other.

Firft, however, I muft ftill venture to make one more material obfervation.

It cannot have efcaped the penetration of a thoughtful mind, on confidering this fub-ject; that, after all, however advantageous the continuance, or even increafe of the National Debt may be, *on account of the increafed circulation of the annual produce of the country in every fhape and mode*; yet that one objec-

F   tion

tion may arife, from the fhare *foreigners* are permitted to have in the funds : who, when *they* receive the interest paid, may carry it entirely out of this country, to be flung into the circulation of property in another country, inftead of being continued here. And who, alfo, in confequence of being permitted to have a vaft degree of property thus vefted, might, on any interefting emergency, greatly depreciate the value of the funds, by felling out immenfe fums. But to this it may furely be anfwered; that, in general, the difadvantage arifing from foreigners having fuch a fhare, is perhaps more than counterbalanced by the advantage which conftantly accrues to *Public credit*, by *their* pouring money and property from abroad, thus continually into the circulation in this country.

And if, at any time, the wifdom of Parliament fhould fee fit to direct the *intereft* paid on any of the great increafing fums, *vefted in the hands of the Commiffioners, for the purpofe of Liquidating the National Debt, to*

ceafe

ceafe being applied to the further liquidation thereof : and inftead of continuing to be added yearly, as it now is; towards *diminifhing* the debt; to be wifely ufed for any other purpofes : *then,* and in fuch cafe ; namely, in any period when the number of *foreign* proprietors of ftock fhould be found on the whole *too great,* and any ways difadvantageous to the country, on the account above mentioned ; the application of the intereft of thofe vaft fums hitherto appropriated to fuch liquidation, might be applied to the paying off *foreign ftockholders,* without any injury to fuch foreigners ; and even with their fulleft approbation ; and to their utmoft fatisfaction : by the commiffioners being impowered, by Parliament, to give public notice of their intention to purchafe *the fhares of foreigners only,* for fome time to come. And then, *after fuch purchafe,* by fuffering the annihilation of fo much ftock to take place, and the intereft to ceafe only there. By this means, *the part of the Debt annihilated* will be continually

that

that alone, the intereft of which was not *in circulation*, in this country.

And even fuppofing that by fuch notice, an opportunity fhould be given to fuch foreigners, to take advantage of the times ; and to make profit; yet it would only make them the more fatisfied to truft us on future emergencies : and the lofs to the Public would be trifling in comparifon of the real gain. And any fteps foreigners might take, if they thought it defirable to do fo, to counteract this meafure, would only tend to raife the value of the remaining Public Funds, and to increafe Public Credit.

Having made this one laft obfervation, I proceed to fuggeft the plain hints I mentioned.

Notwithftanding what has hitherto been fo inadvertently permitted to be done by Provincial Bankers, in getting fuch vaft num- bers of their five guinea, and five pound notes, into circulation, to the amount of fuch an immenfe fum ; nothing can be more clear,

upon

upon the moſt fundamental principles, than
that the iſſuing out of *any notes for general circulation* ought to be as ſacred to Government;
and, under its authority, to thoſe whom it
ſhall depute ; (that is, in the preſent ſtate of
things, *to the Bank of England)* ; as the
iſſuing out of gold or ſilver coin is ſacred
to Government; and to the *Mint at the
tower.*

A contrary ſyſtem has inadvertently been
permitted to go too far. It may, however,
probably, be ſet right even yet, greatly to the
advantage of Government, and for the Public
welfare, by degrees.

Conſidering therefore *Government,* and the
Bank of England, as *one body*; or at leaſt as
cloſely united in one common intereſt : what
I would venture, in the firſt place, to propoſe
is as follows.—

· I do not mean to propoſe, that any ſtep ſhould
be directly taken to controul, or to reſtrain
ſuch Provincial bankers, as can by the aid
now held out keep their ground; but I wiſh

to

to propose, that Government should, by act of Parliament, establish *henceforth a public banking house* in each of the several great provincial cities and towns; under the conduct and direction of Commissioners, or Governors, and of proper public officers, to conduct the business; in the same manner as the business is conducted at the Bank of England; and with the same caution; and under the same kind of controul. And that these banks should have the power of issuing out, under the sanction *of Government*, and *the Bank of England*, five pound, and five guinea notes; for value received: to be in perpetual circulation, like bank notes.

These banks would be no more an infringement on the remaining profits or advantages of the Provincial bankers, than the setting up of any *new banker* in each town at any time is. Which is continually done at pleasure: and has ever been deemed an advantage to the Public circulation. And the superior credit, and security of such *Public Bank*

Bank Notes, would foon caufe them, of courfe, to be *preferred*; and filently to come into general ufe, more than the Provincial bankers notes; and would give the Provincial bankers time to retire, and to fecure their acquirements.

And then, after that, as the next ftep: if the Provincial Bankers notes do not of themfelves, and without any noticebeing taken of them, go out of ufe, and fo leave the greateft benefit of this increafed fund to Government: and if others will ftill venture to increafe fuch impofition on the public; then the next ftep, in due time, may be, for Parliament *to prohibit any notes for general circulation*, to be at all iffued out, except by Government, and the Bank of England; juft as gold or filver coin is prohibited to be coined for circulation, except by public authority: but at the fame time allowing all drafts upon Provincial bankers, fuch as are now drawn upon bankers in London, to pafs from hand to hand, juft as they now do: which kind of

drafts

drafts will, in reality, be fufficient to fupport all the *juft* advantages and profits of the Provincial bankers, upon exactly the fame fcale with the prefent advantages of bankers, in the moft capital banking houfes in London.

And, after fuch prohibition, *let all notes* FOR GENERAL CIRCULATION *be taken from* the offices of Government, and the Bank of England *only, for value paid down in cafh,* juft as bank notes are taken out from the Bank of England.

By this means, the whole *power of coining and iffuing notes* will be henceforth referved, as it ought to be, to Government; and to its proper agent, *the National Bank of England;* juft as *coining* of money is kept facred to Government; and to its proper agent, in that inftance, the *Mint,* in the tower. A power moft neceffary to be referved, in this manner, for the facred firm eftablifhment of all private property. And all the advantage of the vaft fums *funded*

virtually

virtually by the iffuing out of notes needful
for the increafed and increafing circulation
of property; and the fyftem of things that
will gradually take place by this means; will
facilitate the bringing to pafs *that defirable
great event*; which is indeed haftening for-
wards even of itfelf; and which will in the
end be found the greateft and beft fecurity
of all private property; *the rendering the*
WHOLE *a matter of public and moft certain
account.* The final accomplifhment of which
event, is a thing that will be above all
others, furely, the moft confiftent with the
true abftract idea of fecure and permanent
property,

In the next place, it may now be fuggefted,
as a matter well deferving the confideration of
the legiflature AT THIS ALARMING CRISIS;
whether it may not become expedient, on fuch
a great emergency as the prefent, to depart
from the rule, *fo lately eftablifhed,* of appro-
priating a certain fum annually, for what is
called the liquidation of the National Debt:—

G   *and*

and *instead of that appropriation, to direct* THAT VERY SUM *to be appropriated, for a year or two, through the medium of the Bank of England, for the purpose of increasing a more extensive and free circulation of five pound bank notes, to supply the present deficiency of currency; by means of lending such five pound notes to a certain amount,* TO THE SEVERAL CORPORATIONS *of great manufacturing towns,* UPON SUFFICIENT SECURITY FOR PAYING THE INTEREST OF THEM ONLY, AT SOME FIXED ADEQUATE RATE, FOR EVER, AS A STATED REVENUE; UNLESS THEY ARE ABLE, AND VOLUNTARILY CHOOSE, TO PAY OFF THE PRINCIPAL.

AND UPON SECURITY, THAT THEY WILL FROM YEAR TO YEAR, FOR EVER DURING THE SAID SUMS BEING CONTINUED IN THEIR HANDS, EMPLOY THE SAID BANK NOTES, AND THEIR AMOUNT, SO ADVANCED BY GOVERNMENT, ONLY IN DISCOUNTING THE BILLS OF PERSONS OF CREDIT, ACTUALLY ENGAGED IN THE SEVERAL

BRANCHES OF TRADE IN EACH OF THOSE
RESPECTIVE MANUFACTURING TOWNS;
*at such easy rates, as may merely be sufficient to
raise a proper income for paying the appointed
interest to Government; and for paying the
stipends of such officers and clerks as shall be
found needful to transact the business.*

And, at the same time, in order to prevent
any dangerous, or infidious *run* upon the
Bank, in consequence of this increase of
notes; *to declare, by Act of Parliament, all
notes of the Bank of England, to be lawful
current payment, without discount, the same as
gold and silver coin is.*

If such a step as this is taken; even in case
the principal money, so lent, is never paid
by the respective corporations; yet the
money so lent, and which is now applied
merely to the liquidation of the National
'Debt, will never be materially missed: and
will be applied *to at least as beneficial a purpose
as it now is:*—and *the annual interest* of the
money *so lent*, will become no inconsiderable
object to Government.

A better plan may perhaps be devifed :—
but the circulation of fmall bank notes, more
largely, and freely, *under the authority of
Government, and the Crown, as a real fpecies
of coin*, becomes more and more neceffary
every day.

This medium of the Bank, authorized by
the Crown, and by Parliament; *and thefe
notes from* ONE *fource only*; ought ever, it
fhould feem, to be *the unfhaken fource of the
circulation* of all folid property; as much as
the Mint in the tower, and gold and filver
coinage is : *which latter fpecies of circulation
alone* can never afford a fufficient currency in
this great and commercial kingdom.

A circulation of currency *more freely* in
fome fhape or other, proportionable to the
immenfe property it contains, this country
muft have; or elfe its wealth muft ftagnate;
its operations and energy be ftifled;—and it
muft perifh.—

The danger and mifchief *of felf-created
currency*, without proper funds, is now
generally felt.—There is danger, alfo, *more*

than I can properly *exprefs* (or *choofe properly to exprefs*, on this occafion), *in the mere paper currency of an unfunded debt:*—as there is alfo *a want* of its being fufficiently extenfive; or (which is more to the purpofe), fufficiently fubdivided into fmall fums.

The real relief, therefore, muft be *an extenfion of currency*; only with fufficient funds and ftability. A currency of the fame kind in effect, but far beyond it in ftable fupport, with that, which has fo fadly, and fo rafhly been lately, in a private manner, *attempted*; and fo inadvertently *permitted* to go forth in the country at large; without fuch fufficient funds and ability.

The Crown, with the advice of the legiflature; and by its fole proper inftrument, *the Bank of England* (through whofe hands *muft ever unavoidably pafs* the greateft part of all *perfonal property*; which muft ever increafe far beyond the *poffibility of the extent* of any other property); *The Crown can alone* give fuffi-cient ftability, and fupport to this moft neceffary

part

part of the *vital motion*, in the Body Politic.
—and for want alone of the support of this
vital motion and circulation, there is *now*
danger of such *a mortification*, and stagnation;
as must bring on *diffolution*; as effectually as
a mortification does in the natural body.

This country is, in reality, in this
instance, somewhat in danger of suffering, if
not even of perishing, by a political mortification.

The wisdom of Parliament, we have every
reason to believe, will *finally* adopt some
method of relief, more advantageous and
effectual than can be suggested by any private
individual.—But, whilst I express the most
earnest wishes for *such* relief, I may venture to
add, that there is not surely any danger that
the adopting such a *method of redress* as I have
ventured to propose, should be injurious;
either by promoting a mere *paper currency*; or
by giving an opportunity, at any future time,
for *a run* either upon the Bank in London,
or upon the Government Banking houses in
the

the country : becaufe, in reality, *a paper currency* does now, at this prefent moment, actually take place, even *under the moft difadvantageous circumftances* ; as much as it ever can do *under the moft advantageous circumftances.*

This, every man who receives rents, or the iffues of any property either in the country, or by remittances *from* the country, in any part of this kingdom, can teftify. And it is moft true, that even this fort of *paper currency,* (thus imprudently allowed, on the foundation only of accident, and for the fake of fupporting merely the private interefts of Provincial bankers, without any proper funds) has yet proved not only of great advantage to the public for a time; inftead of being of any detriment ; but of *fo much advantage;* that the country cannot well contrive to do without it : or indeed at all carry on its commerce, and ufual inter-courfe, without fomething fimilar fubftituted in its room.

Let

Let us, therefore, ere it be too late, allow ourſelves to think very cloſely and deeply on the ſubject; and to lay aſide inveterate prejudices; and to free ourſelves from deeply rivetted, mere popular errors.

The true intereſt of a country can never conſiſt in cheriſhing even the leaſt of ſuch errors; any more than the perfection of man's underſtanding conſiſts in cheriſhing the imaginations of childhood.

Let us, cautiouſly, inſtead of being guilty of ſuch inadvertency, exert ourſelves, guarding diligently againſt the inſidious arts of thoſe who would, at any time, avail themſelves of ſuch popular prejudices, and of temporary accidents, to deceive: and thankfully conſidering, as we ought, that Almighty God has indeed beſtowed innumerable, and, if it be not our own fault, inexhauſtible bleſſings upon this country.

We may, by wickedneſs, blundering, and error, become *felo de ſe*: but we may boldly truſt, upon the moſt rational grounds, and

froɾe

from every appearance of things ; that if we do not forfake God, and by neglecting to ufe our underftanding aright, feek our own ruin, He will not forfake us ; nor withdraw His fupport from our affectionate and gracious Sovereign, who has fo conftantly ftudied to make his welfare confift in the welfare of his people. Neither will the Almighty Goodnefs fuffer a land, whofe inhabitants will but continue to be induftrious, and fincere, to be confounded; but it is to be hoped will yet, of His great Mercy, blefs fuch land with continued profperity.

THE END:

www.ingramcontent.com/pod-product-compliance
Lightning Source LLC
Chambersburg PA
CBHW021641270326
41931CB00008B/1108